T0017064

THE
GHOSTLY TALES
OF
SAN JOSE

Published by Arcadia Children's Books
A Division of Arcadia Publishing
Charleston, SC
www.arcadiapublishing.com

Spooky America is a trademark of Arcadia Publishing, Inc.

First published 2024

Manufactured in the United States

ISBN 978-1-4671-9756-4

Library of Congress Control Number: 2023950128

Designed by Jessica Nevins
Images used courtesy of Shutterstock.com; p. 6 fivetonine/Shutterstock.com;
p. 20 DreamArt123/Shutterstock.com; p. 66 Wangkun JiaShutterstock.com.

Notice: The information in this book is true and complete to the best of our
knowledge. It is offered without guarantee on the part of the author or Arcadia
Publishing. The author and Arcadia Publishing disclaim all liability in connection with
the use of this book.

Spooky America

THE GHOSTLY TALES OF

SAN JOSE

ANNA LARDINOIS

Adapted from Haunted San Jose By Elizabeth Kile

arcadia
CHILDREN'S BOOKS

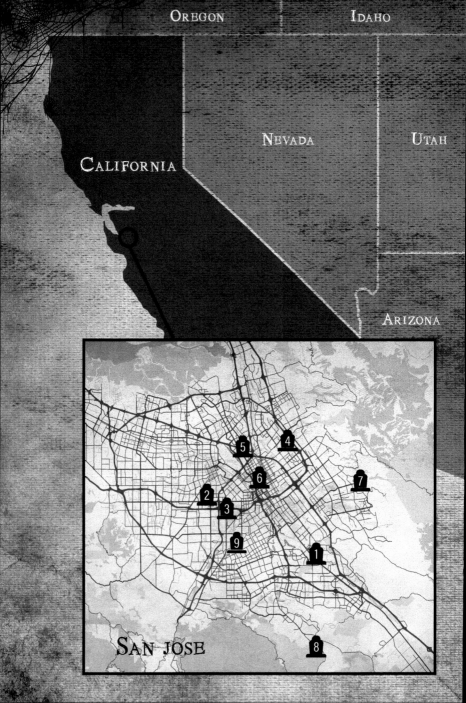

TABLE OF CONTENTS & MAP KEY

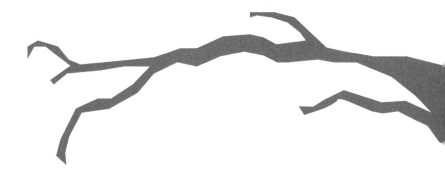

Welcome to Spooky San Jose!

There is no doubt about it—San Jose is one spooky city!

San Jose is the largest city in Santa Clara County. And some think it is also the most haunted! The city was founded in 1777, but the tales of strange happenings in the area go back even further.

The city is famous for many things. It was California's first state capital. It is the home of

Silicon Valley and the world's largest Monopoly board. And, the city's ghosts are going to knock your socks off!

In this book, we'll take a look at some of San Jose's most spooktacular spirits. Together, we will explore the Winchester Mystery House®, discovering why it was under construction for thirty-eight years, and why more than twelve million people have toured this strange house!

We'll also take a look at a cemetery so terrifying, we probably shouldn't have included it in this collection of stories. There is an otherworldly entity so frightening that it is practically *guaranteed* to give you nightmares.

Other tales included in this book feature spine-tingling schools, theaters where the show continues after death, and a hotel where a few of the former guests have never checked out. Not to mention, a haunted house that looks just like any other house. Well, on the

outside. The *inside* is a completely different story . . .

So, are you ready to meet San Jose's ghosts? If so, turn the page. That is, if you dare to encounter the amazingly abundant paranormal activity lurking in the shadows of San Jose.

Hayes Mansion

Mystical Mary and Her Mansion

The Hayes Mansion has a strange history.

If you've ever gone to the Edenvale Gardens Regional Park on the south side of the city, you have probably seen the Hayes Mansion. The large Spanish revival building with a red tile roof sits just outside the park. Built in 1905 as a home for the Hayes family, today this stunning structure serves as a hotel. But the most famous member of the Hayes family never lived in the home. Well . . . at least not while she was alive.

Mary Hayes-Chynoweth was meant to live in the elegant mansion's sixty-four rooms with her grown sons, Jay and Everis, and their families. Mary should have played in the home's grand solarium with her grandchildren and strolled through the marble-tiled hallways, but she never got the chance.

Mary might not have lived in the famous mansion named after her family, but she did live on the property. Previously, the family had had a huge 22,000 square-foot mansion on the land. They lived there for eight years before fire destroyed the home. In 1903, the family started construction on what is now the Hayes Mansion. Mary watched while the grand home was being built, but she died before the home was completed.

You might be wondering where the family's

wealth came from, wealth that allowed them to build a home so large it once had its own post office and railway station. The answer will probably surprise you.

Mary had psychic healing powers. At least, that is what she, and her many followers, believed.

Her otherworldly powers revealed themselves when she was a young woman in Wisconsin. At the time, she was a schoolteacher. But in 1853, something happened that changed her life forever.

Mary was carrying a basin of water in her kitchen when a strange feeling came over her. She felt what she described as a "force" push her to her knees. Instantly, she was kneeling on the floor of the kitchen and unable to move. She lost her ability to see. She could not use her voice to speak. She was helpless.

Suddenly, Mary felt her mouth and tongue

move. She heard her voice speaking unfamiliar words in a language she did not understand. During this astounding experience, she received a message from the "force" that held her to the kitchen floor. The message told her that she should spend the rest of her life serving others, using her powers for healing through spiritual medicine.

Mary listened to the voice and began to heal the sick. She strongly believed the ability to perform these amazing feats came directly from God. She traveled from town to town, preaching the word of God while performing extraordinary acts of healing. It has been said she could even see inside of people, detecting tumors and other internal problems well before X-rays were invented! People were in awe of her abilities.

Mary was now able to heal the sick with

just a touch of her hand. Her new powers gave her other unexplained talents as well. She was able to speak and understand languages she had never known before. And she could even predict future events.

Those predictions would prove to be very profitable for Mary's family.

In 1882, the "force" instructed Mary and her sons to invest in a plot of land in northern Wisconsin. Guided by nothing but her belief, she purchased the land and discovered a rich vein of iron ore on the property. Her sons started a mining company and the family soon became rich.

In 1887, the family was wealthy enough to leave snowy Wisconsin and move to sunny California. Mary and her sons, along with many people who admired Mary's otherworldly talents, made their home in San Jose, in a colony called Edenvale. Mary established the True Life Church of San Jose on the property and used it as a place to talk about God and the miraculous powers that had been given to her.

Thousands of people from all over the world traveled to Edenvale with the hope that Mary would cure the diseases that ailed them. Visitors to Edenvale told astonishing tales of Mary's ability to heal people whom doctors previously had claimed were incurable. Eyewitnesses reported seeing people who hobbled in on crutches throw their crutches on the ground and begin to dance!

After years of healing and teaching others about her mysterious abilities, Mary died in 1905. Eventually, the Hayes family sold their massive home, and it became a hotel and convention center in 1994.

Now that you know a bit about the history of the house and Mary's life, it probably won't surprise you to learn that many people think the Hayes mansion, and the land it sits on, is haunted.

Guests of the Hayes Mansion have told stories of paranormal happenings in the hotel for years.

Those who venture into the oldest part of the hotel report the feeling of being watched. Unseen eyes follow guests as they walk through what was once the Hayes family home.

Late at night—far past the bedtimes of boys and girls still among the living—children can be heard playing in the hallways of the hotel. Laughter echoes through the empty corridors as sounds of small footsteps race past the doors of sleeping guests. Several people have reported seeing the apparition of a youngster pedaling a tricycle through the hallways. Who are these children who continue to use the hotel as a playground in the afterlife?

No one knows. But we do know the spirits of the children are not the only ghosts that have made the Hayes Mansion their home.

Danny Diaz and his wife stayed in the hotel in 2005. Their experience just might convince you that the building is haunted. *Extremely* haunted.

As soon as Danny and his wife arrived at the hotel, they felt uncomfortable. While walking around the place, they had the sensation of being watched. As the couple's unease grew, they decided to speak with the front desk clerk. To their relief, the clerk explained that their room was in the new part of the hotel, behind the building that was once the Hayes family home. Their room, he assured them, was not haunted. They had nothing to worry about.

Danny and his wife returned to their room and tried to relax. But the clerk, it turned out, was wrong.

Very wrong.

At three in the morning, a loud crash in the room startled them awake. Shaken, Danny jumped out of his bed to find the source of the noise. He found it in the bathroom.

Somehow, a lightbulb had fallen from the bathroom ceiling and crashed on the tile floor below. It was strange enough that the light bulb could somehow unscrew itself, but when

Danny bent over to pick up the pieces of the broken bulb, he couldn't find any!

Instead of the shards of glass Danny expected to find all over the bathroom floor, he saw that the glass bulb had pulverized into a fine dust. Danny was puzzled as to how this had happened. He called the front desk and asked to have someone come to the room and help him clean the bathroom and replace the light bulb.

When the hotel's maintenance man arrived, he looked scared. The man's hands were shaking as he entered the room. It was obvious he did not want to be there. He was afraid of what he believed to be inside.

The man explained to Danny and his wife that they were in danger. Based on his experience working at the hotel, when something like this happened, it was the work of a bad spirit. He believed a bad spirit was in the room with them. As his shaking hands swept the pulverized glass from the bathroom floor, he warned the couple to leave the hotel for their own safety. Within moments, Danny and his wife began to pack their bags.

They raced to get out of the hotel as quickly as possible. Even though all the other guests were sleeping, the pair felt like they were being followed. A heavy sense of dread surrounded them. They could still feel unseen eyes upon them as they rushed out the door toward the parking lot. When they finally reached their car, they turned around to look back at the hotel.

What they saw made them gasp in fright.

The building was blanketed in darkness. Not a single light shone in any window. They knew something wasn't right as they opened the car doors and got in their vehicle. They felt relief as they drove away.

Just who or what was after them that night is still a mystery to Danny and his wife. With the strange history of the building and its

surrounding property, the hotel's otherworldly entity could be any number of terrifying things. Whatever it was, they felt it was evil and meant them harm.

While this event remains a mystery, the one thing the couple knows for certain is that they will never, *ever*, go back to the Hayes Mansion. And, frankly, I don't blame them a bit. How about you? What would it take to get you to spend the night in the Hayes Mansion?

Winchester Mystery House®

Sarah Winchester's Mysterious House

The Winchester Mystery House® is one of the most famous homes in the San Jose area. Sarah Winchester's former home is massive! The mansion is more than 24,000 square feet and contains "10,000 windows, 2,000 doors, 160 rooms, 52 skylights, 47 stairways and fireplaces, 17 chimneys, 13 bathrooms, and 6 kitchens."

But it's not just the size of the house that gives it its claim to fame. The strange reason why it has so many elements have added to the house's reputation and mystery. Oh, and the ghosts. Don't forget about the ghosts!

Sarah Winchester, who built the house, has become a bit of a legend in San Jose, and some of what you might hear about her is fiction. But here are the facts: Sarah Pardee was born in New Haven, Connecticut, in 1839. In 1862, she married William Wirt Winchester. William's father, Oliver Winchester, founded

the Winchester Repeating Arms Company. The company was a very successful gun manufacturer. It made the Winchester Model 1873 Rifle, which was marketed as "the gun that won the West."

Four years after Sarah and William married, Sarah gave birth to a baby girl, whom they named Annie. The new baby was doted on by both her parents. Sadly, the little girl's life was cut short. Annie became ill and died when she was just six weeks old. Her parents were devastated.

After the death of her daughter, Sarah was never quite the same. She grieved the loss of her baby for the rest of her life.

William's father, Oliver, passed away in December 1880 and, just a few months later, William died from tuberculosis. (Tuberculosis is an infection caused by bacteria. It usually infects the lungs, but it can also affect the kidneys, spine, and brain.) With the death of her husband and father-in-law, Sarah inherited a fifty percent stake in the Winchester Repeating Arms Company, making her one of the wealthiest women in the country. (Some sources claim that her daily income was $1,000, which would be around $25,000 today.) However, she was all alone in the world. So, Sarah decided to move to San Jose to be closer to her sister.

When Sarah arrived in San Jose, she bought an eight-room farmhouse on forty acres of land. Nothing mysterious about that. That is, until she decided to . . . expand the house.

Legend has it that construction went on in the house twenty-four hours a day, three hundred sixty-five days a year for the next twenty years! The sound of hammers pounding

and saws tearing through wood could be heard around the clock. Sarah added room after room, as well as new staircases and additional doorways.

The grieving widow didn't just want her new home to be big—she wanted it to be beautiful! She purchased glittering chandeliers to light her new rooms. She installed custom made stained glass throughout the house. No expense was spared. But the work was never complete. There was always something new being built at the Winchester mansion.

Before long, townspeople began to talk about some of the unusual things Sarah had built in her home. They whispered about doors that led to nowhere. They wondered why the woman would have a staircase built that ended at the ceiling. And everyone speculated about the small room in the center of the home with two doors: one to enter, and the other to exit. All this gossip helped create the home's mysterious reputation.

Some believe the reason behind all the construction is something otherworldly. It has been said that a psychic medium influenced Sarah to build her massive, mysterious house. (A medium is a person who claims that they can communicate with the souls of people who have passed away.)

A movement called Spiritualism became popular in the United States in the late 1800s. A key belief of the movement was that spirits of the dead could communicate with the living. Psychic mediums played a large role in Spiritualism because they claimed to be able to communicate directly with these spirits.

Mediums used all kinds of different methods to speak with the dead. Some would claim to go into a trance and let the spirits of the dead  speak through them. Others would conduct seances to encourage the restless spirits to send messages via ouija boards (wooden boards with letters printed on them that people use to contact the spirit world) or make noises to speak from beyond the grave.

Many people believe that Sarah visited a famous psychic medium named Adam Coons after her husband died. He supposedly had a startling message for Sarah Winchester: not only was her family cursed, but the souls of all the people ever killed by Winchester rifles were destined to haunt Sarah forever.

Coons may have even told Sarah that her daughter and husband had died not because of illness, but because of the terrible curse upon the family. If Sarah wanted to avoid the curse, she would need to do something to save herself.

The psychic medium advised Sarah that to stay safe, she must build her house in a way that would confuse, and even trap, the angry spirits. To do this, she must continue construction on her home. The bigger and more complicated her home was, the harder it would be for the tormented souls to find her.

It is said that Sarah believed if construction ended on her home, the spirits she eluded would finally catch up to and ultimately kill her!

So, it's no wonder the house is so massive and that there are countless rooms, zigzagging stairways that suddenly stop, and thousands of doors to nowhere! (Including one on the second floor that opens to the outside—a dangerous drop for anyone who steps through it!)

If you believe the legends, there are just about as many ghosts in the old house as there are rooms in the Winchester Mystery House®. In addition to the spirits of those killed by Winchester rifles, some say the house is also haunted by workers who are still on the job . . . even in the afterlife.

Mansion employees often spot the ghost

of a man wearing overalls and a cap roaming the grounds. They believe the ghost is the spirit of the home's former caretaker, whom the employees have named Clyde. Apparently, Clyde is still going about his duties, even though his employer died more than one hundred years ago!

Clyde is not the only entity from beyond the grave that people claim to see lurking around the home. A petite older woman with gray hair is frequently spotted on the grounds. Many believe this is the ghost of Sarah Winchester herself! People have also reported seeing the

imprint of a human figure lying in Sarah's bed in the room where she died. Creepy!

Then there are the dark shadowy figures known to slink down dark hallways, and the unexplained cold spots visitors experience while touring the house. Empty rocking chairs gently rock back and forth on their own. Unseen hands turn doorknobs, opening and closing doors though there's no soul in sight.

Well, no *living* soul, that is.

Maybe scariest of all are the sounds echoing through the house. Mysterious footsteps. Creaking floorboards. Voices and laughter coming from empty rooms.

How is that possible?

Employees and visitors also claim to have seen orbs at the Winchester Mystery House®. Orbs are glowing balls of light believed to be the manifestation of energy. Some people believe this energy comes from ghosts or spirits. Orbs can be large or small, and the living may sometimes see orbs without any special equipment. Other times, these balls of light reveal themselves in photographs.

Today, the Winchester Mystery House® is a popular tourist attraction. People come from all over the world to see the strange house for themselves. A man named Allen Weitzel used to be a manager at the house. One of his jobs was to lock up at the end of the day. After all the tours had ended and all the other employees had gone home, Allen would walk through the house and make sure the place was empty. He'd lock all the doors and turn off all the lights, then head to the gift shop at the front gate. There, Allen would turn on the security alarm, double check that everything was secure, and leave for the night.

One evening, after Allen had gone through his usual closing routine, he turned back to look at the house before heading to the parking lot. The house was completely dark, just as it should be.

When Allen reached his car, he turned around to look at the house one more time. Imagine his shock when he saw that all of the lights on the third floor had suddenly flickered on!

As he watched the light glow from the windows, Allen wondered how it was possible. He had been the last person in the building. He'd set the security system with his own hands. If anyone else had been in the building, they would have set off the alarm.

Allen is not the only person who has had an eerie experience connected with the third floor of the house. Once, a tour guide was on the third floor when he heard footsteps coming down the hall. He looked out of the doorway and saw a figure a few feet away from him. The tour guide thought he was seeing a visitor or another employee and decided to say hello to the person. However, as the tour guide approached the figure, it slowly disappeared right before his eyes.

Later, the tour guide realized that the house had not been open for tours when he'd spotted the disappearing figure, so there was no way it could have been another employee or a visitor.

So just who—or *what*—was that figure he saw?

Writer and author of *Haunted San Jose*, Elizabeth Kile, had her own spinetingling experience when she went on a behind-the-scenes tour of the Winchester Mystery House®. On that day, Elizabeth's tour guide had led the small tour group into the basement. Even though dim light shone in from the basement windows, the room was very dark. The tour guide had a flashlight and kept the beam of light on the floor so the group could see where they were walking.

When the group reached a large room, the tour guide paused for a moment and turned off

her flashlight. In the murky dark, she began to talk about ghost sightings in the basement.

As soon as the guide mentioned that Clyde was often seen in the basement, Elizabeth noticed something strange. About twenty feet behind the tour guide, Elizabeth spotted a circle of light. She watched the light bounce along the wall, near the ceiling. She asked her friend standing next to her if she saw the bouncing light, too. She did! The women watched the light bounce a few more times before it disappeared entirely.

Elizabeth was puzzled. She knew the light she saw could not have come from the basement windows. She could also see for herself that no one in the group had a flashlight or any other way to project light on the basement wall.

Had Elizabeth and her friend witnessed one of the supernatural orbs that other visitors had reported seeing? And if so, was it the spirit of Clyde letting the tour group know he was with them? If it wasn't Clyde, then who? Perhaps one of the restless spirits known to search for Sarah in her mysterious house? Or maybe it

was Sarah herself, keeping a watchful eye on wandering visitors?

Just who, or what, haunts the Winchester Mystery House® may never be known. But whatever is there seems to want to interact with the living. Are you brave enough to pay a visit and find out if the spirits that still linger want to connect with *you*?

Del Mar High School's Fearsome Football Field

Have you heard the spooky story about Del Mar High School? Legend has it that the school's football field is haunted!

The land that the school now stands on was once covered by fruit orchards. The story goes that back in 1942, two young men, who were best friends, were in the orchard long past midnight. At some point in the night, the pair began to argue. Soon, the argument became a physical fight, and before long, one of the young men lay dead on the ground beneath the fruit trees.

By 1957, the dead man had been forgotten and the orchard cut down. The city decided to build Del Mar High School, along with its football field, on the now vacant land. When

the school opened in 1959, the students who walked through its doors had no idea that someone had died on the Del Mar High School grounds.

People may have forgotten the dead man, but it wasn't long before his spirit reminded them that he had met a tragic end on the site. And, if you believe the stories...he is *still* there.

Generations of students have reported particularly strange phenomena at the football field. Some have seen the figure of a person running up and down the field's bleachers in the middle of the night. Many have claimed to hear cries for help coming from the empty field at 3:15 in the morning, the exact time when the young man was reportedly murdered. Those who've heard the voice calling out in the middle of the night often go looking for the person pleading for help . . . but never find another soul in the football field.

Even the birds seem to know something strange is happening in that field. A murder of crows (a murder is what they call a group of crows—scary, right?) regularly gathers to keep watch, their jet-black feathers glinting in the sun as they circle the field. The birds' shrill cries fill the air, warning all those in the area that something in this field is amiss.

After years of rumored hauntings, a paranormal investigation was conducted in and around the football field. The ghost hunters performed an EVP test in the field. EVP stands for Electronic Voice Phenomenon, and the tests are conducted to capture noises or sounds supposedly made by spirits. Investigators listen to the recordings in the hope that they will hear sounds not detected by their ears. One of the ghost hunters said, "We just want to know why you're here," out into the empty football field.

Unbelievably, the recorder picked up a response. Investigators heard someone clearly say, "OK" to the ghost hunter.

Just who responded remains a mystery. The investigators are certain it was not a member of their team. Most who learn of the recording believe it was the voice of the man who died on the site in 1942.

This paranormal activity continues to this day. The murdered man remains tied to the land, making himself known to those brave—or foolish—enough to seek him out in the early morning hours.

Do you want your *own* ghostly encounter enough to visit the deserted football field in the darkest part of the night and call out to the long dead man? Or, is it better not to know the tales this spirit seems to want to tell?

Hooray for School Spirit!

What comes to mind when someone mentions the term "school spirit?" Most people think of school assemblies, cheering on your school's teams, and school mascots.

Well, that is not the case for students at Independence High School. When you say "school spirit'" at the largest high school in San Jose, chances are the first thing students think of is George. *Who's George?* you might ask. Well,

George is the name of the ghost that reportedly haunts the theater at Independence High!

No one knows for sure who the spirit in the theater was in life, or why he is there. In fact, his name probably isn't even George. Years ago, Kellye Dodd, a dance teacher at the school who has experienced numerous strange events, is the person who gave the ghost his name. Generations of students have claimed the ghost is a janitor who fell to his death from the catwalk high above the stage. But Kellye says this story is not true.

While the story of how the theater got its

very own ghost remains a mystery, there is no denying there is an otherworldly presence. George is rarely ever seen, but he definitely makes himself known.

The spirit can be heard walking on the catwalks above the stage or banging on the walls of the theater. Sometimes, George likes to play with the lights. One of his favorite things to do is startle theater classes by turning the lights off and temporarily plunging them into darkness. (Don't worry—George always turns the lights back on. But not before giving everyone a good scare!)

No one knows exactly what George looks like, but they have seen a shadowy being they believe to be him. The ghostly figure of a man has been spotted moving past the box office and inside the control booth. Some people who have seen the mysterious form have tried to take a closer look at it, but they have been unsuccessful. When a person looks directly at the entity, it disappears just as quickly as it appeared. Eerie, right?!

George is also active in the theater office. He is known to move objects around, leaving teachers searching for items that were on their desks just moments before. One teacher had a bone-chilling encounter with George as she opened the door to the office. She was about to step into the room when she felt a burst of cold air rush past her and down the hall. There was nothing in the office that could have created the strong gust of wind that swept past her.

This experience is even stranger if you know that many people believe a sudden drop in temperature can indicate that a spirit is present. If you have ever discovered a cold spot in a room, or felt an icy breeze drift over you unexpectedly, you may have had your own paranormal encounter! The teacher walking into the empty office certainly believes that is what she experienced when she opened the door.

George may strike you as spooky, but it appears he has a bit of a sense of humor—as well as some very specific taste in music. This ghost does *not* like the music of Michael Jackson. Students claim whenever the theater plays a song by the "King of Pop," George will fast-forward through the song.

I guess everyone is a critic, even from beyond the grave!

Sometimes George even likes to be part of the audience. There is a seat in the theater, usually the same one, that folds down as if someone is sitting in it, watching rehearsals or performances.

Once, a staff member brought his dog along to a rehearsal of *Macbeth*, a play by William Shakespeare. Rather than exploring the theater or sniffing around backstage, the dog went directly to "George's seat" and

sat down in front of it. The dog stared at the seemingly empty chair for the entire rehearsal and sometimes let out a high pitch whine. This went on for hours. The dog would not move from the seat and its whining grew louder throughout the evening.

But then, out of nowhere, the seat of the chair suddenly flipped back up, seemingly on its own! The dog stopped whining and trotted down the aisle of the theater, calmly wagging its tail, as if nothing had happened at all.

(Talk about *paws-itively* spooky!)

Exactly what was in that chair that bothered the dog so much? And where did it go?

Paranormal investigators spent hours in the school in 2009, and they had an interesting experience in the theater. They searched every inch of the theater, including the office, looking for George. They did not find evidence of George, but they *did* detect something on an EVP recording. When the investigators listened to the audio recording of the session, they heard what they believed to be a distinct voice.

A breathy voice said, "Matthew." It was all they heard, but it was enough for them to suspect an unseen presence was with them in the theater.

No one knows who Matthew is, or if it was George who whispered the name into

the recorder, but everyone who enters the Independence High School Theater is sure it is haunted. *Very* haunted.

So, how is that for school spirit?

CHAPTER
5

The Mystery of Room 538

The hotel room on the fifth floor of the Holiday Inn Silicon Valley might look like any other room in the hotel. But looks can be deceiving. Many believe it is the most haunted hotel room in all of San Jose.

The haunting goes back to the early days of the hotel. When it opened in 1974, it was known as the Le Baron Hotel. It was considered one of the most modern and luxurious hotels in San Jose.

Shortly after the hotel opened, a traveling salesman arrived at the Le Baron after a long day of work. The exhausted man was given room 538. He grabbed the key from the front desk clerk and headed up to the fifth floor.

It was the last time he was ever seen alive.

When morning arrived, the man did not check out of his hotel room. Calls to the room went unanswered. The hotel staff knocked on the door but got no response. Concerned, a hotel worker used a passkey to open the locked door.

When they walked into the room, they understood right away why the man had not checked out of room 538 that morning. He was lying on the bed—dead. He was still wearing the dark suit he'd had on when he checked into the hotel. The employees ran from the room in shock! They could not believe what they had just seen. They immediately called the police, and soon, the dead man was removed from the hotel.

But that was not the last time the hotel employees saw the man.

Today, fifty years after his death, the spirit of the man who died in room 538 continues to linger in the place where he took his final breath. Members of the housekeeping staff report terrifying encounters with his ghost, still wearing the same rumpled dark suit, when they come into the room to clean it. There is no mistaking what they see. The man appears as a full-body apparition, not just a shadowy figure passing through a wall or breezing past an open doorway.

Hotel guests unlucky enough to spend the night in room 538 report similarly frightening tales. Lights flicker on and off by themselves. The radio in the room seems to have a mind of its own, turning on and off and changing stations without being touched. Unless . . . could it be an unseen hand controlling the radio? Other overnight guests have heard unexplained noises in the room that left them trembling in fear and counting the seconds until check-out time.

But there's plenty more spookiness where that came from. Doors in the room slam shut

without earthly intervention. Water faucets turn on and off in the seemingly empty bathroom. Even the elevator has been known to travel up to the fifth floor and mysteriously stop—without anybody inside. It certainly appears that whatever entity resides here has a message for the living: When you stay in room 538, you are not alone!

You might be thinking: *No problem, I'll just stay in a different room!* Well, think again! Hotel employees and guests have seen the ghostly man in the dark suit roaming the dining room, too. Not to mention wandering the hallways on the fourth, fifth, and sixth floors of the hotel. But wait—there's more!

A newspaper article that ran in the February 3, 1982 edition of the *San Jose Mercury News* tells the story of a young woman who died in room 538 in 1979. Several months after the woman died, hotel housekeeper Lupe Moncivais had an experience in the room that left her terrified.

When Lupe entered the room to clean it, she heard a voice. It was very faint, as if the voice were coming from far away. She strained to hear what the voice said. And what she heard made her freeze. It was calling her name! "Lupe. *Lupe*," the soft voice said.

At first, Lupe thought her coworkers were playing a joke on her. But moments later, when she heard the voice whisper in her ear as if it wanted to ask her something, she knew this was no joke.

The trembling housekeeper then felt invisible fingers run through her hair. The

fingers grabbed hold of her hair and gave it a sharp tug! Can you imagine? The pain from her hair being pulled told Lupe that something otherworldly was definitely in the room with her!

Another housekeeper was working on the fifth floor when she noticed a woman walking into room 538. The housekeeper thought this was strange, because she knew the room

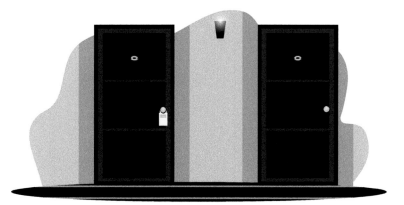

was unoccupied. Then she noticed that the woman in the doorway . . . was *shimmering*. The housekeeper shivered in fear as she watched the glowing form of a woman enter the hotel room!

Might the deaths in room 538 have anything to do with the hotel's haunted elevator? Time

and time again, the empty elevator car rises mysteriously to the fifth floor. The doors open on floor five, but no one is inside the car. Well, at least no one who can be *seen*.

Could it be one of the hotel's ghostly guests returning to room 538? Why have these spirits chosen to remain in the hotel, anyway?

Perhaps the best way to find out is to check into room 538 for yourself. Of course, that is, only if you are eager to spend the night with some *very* bold ghosts!

SAN JOSE IMPROV

MPROV

3-14-16 STEVE TREVINO
3-20-23 ARI SHAFFIR
3-28 CRISTELA ALONZO

San Jose Improv

An Encore for the Jose Theatre

The Jose Theatre (now known as the San Jose Improv) has been a part of the San Jose arts and culture scene since it first opened its doors in 1904. It was a lively place back then. Residents flocked to the theater to see all kinds of entertainment. One week, you could see a serious play, and the next week, a group of dancers might glide across the stage.

There was a seemingly endless rotation of actors, magicians, comedians, and musicians performing at the theater. No matter the day, there was always something happening at the Jose!

When movies arrived on the scene, people lined up to see them. Before long, the theater booked fewer live acts and more movies. Eventually, the only show you could see at the Jose was a movie. The theater showed movies until 1989 when the building was damaged by the Loma Prieta earthquake.

Repairs would be very expensive and the owners were not interested in restoring the building. It seemed as if the doors of the historic theater would remain closed forever. But in 1990, the city of San Jose declared the Jose Theatre a landmark, purchased the building, and began to rebuild the theater.

Today, the building is known as the San Jose Improv. The theater once again features live performers on the stage. Comedians from all over the country travel to San Jose to perform in the theater, just like they did in the early days. The only difference is that today's performers have a slightly different audience. Of course, they have the fans in the seats who purchased tickets. But they *also* have an audience that cannot be detected with the human eye ... an audience some say has been hanging around the theater for more than a century.

That's right—according to locals, it is likely that some of the original performers from the early 1900s never left the building!

Back in 2021, David Williams, the manager of the San Jose Improv, gave an interview about paranormal happenings in the theater. He explained to the podcaster that before he worked in the theater, he did not believe in ghosts. Now he is *certain* that ghosts are real.

David remembers one warm evening when he was in the theater's Green Room. This is the place where performers relax and chat with each other before and after they go on stage. The Green Room felt too hot, so he opened all of the windows to let the breeze cool the room.

David stepped out of the room for a moment. When he returned, he noticed the room was a bit cooler. He was glad he'd opened the windows. He sat down to enjoy the breeze and started doing some paperwork in the empty room. Minutes later, when he looked up from his desk, he noticed something that sent a shiver up his spine.

Every single window in the room was now *closed*!

David's heart began to beat faster. He had not closed the windows. He had been alone in the room the entire time. He had not seen anyone enter the room, and he had not heard the windows close. But somehow, it had happened!

Perhaps the mischievous spirit of one of those performers from long ago was playing tricks on David? Or maybe the spirit just likes the Green Room's windows closed? It is unknown who or what closed those windows, but David is *certain* it was something otherworldly.

The Green Room is not the only place in the theater thought to be haunted. The upper bar seems to have its own ghostly residents. For years, bartenders have noticed that the wine glasses that hang above the bar sometimes rattle and shake for no obvious reason. After ghost hunters investigated the theater's upper bar in 2008, they found paranormal activity a likely source of the unexplained movements.

The hunters captured multiple EVP recordings in the room. One voice they captured was that of a very angry man. The otherworldly man cursed at the investigators and demanded they leave the bar.

That was not the only voice recorded in the room. The investigators also captured the voice of woman. Unlike the ghostly man, her voice was very faint, but she seemed to be responding to the questions the investigators were asking her.

Are these voices from the upper bar the same spirits that still visit the Green Room? If not, can you imagine just how many other spirits might still be haunting the old theater?

There is only one way to find out—visit the theater for yourself. Whether you watch the performance on stage, or you catch a glimpse of something lurking in the shadows, it is bound to be a memorable—and maybe even *spooktacular*—night at the Jose Theatre!

The Quimby Road Jogger

Quimby Road is one of the oldest roads in San Jose. It is also thought to be one of the city's most *haunted* roads. The road gets its creepy reputation because it is the home of one of San Jose's most famous ghosts—the Quimby Road jogger. The ghostly jogger does not appear on the busier parts of Quimby Road, home to shops, schools, and lots of traffic. To find this spirit, you must follow the road into the foothills. As you continue to travel east, the road grows narrower. Farther on your journey, as cars climb the mountain, the guard rail disappears, making the remote road even more dangerous.

It is on this stretch of the winding road where generations of drivers have spotted the spooky specter. The ghostly jogger shows himself at night, most often around midnight. A driver will catch a glimpse of the man in the car's headlight. As the car gets nearer to the otherworldly runner, the ghost will veer off to the side of the road and then disappear into the bushes. After that, there is no trace of the jogger—as if he was never there at all.

Seeing a man appear and disappear on the side of a dark and lonely road sounds scary, but not as scary as some reports that have come from Quimby Road. Some drivers are certain the spirit they have seen jogging alongside the road is missing its head! You may still be deciding whether or not you believe in ghosts. But the headless jogger is *certain* to chill the spine of even the bravest driver on Quimby Road.

Some say you don't need to be in a car to see the Quimby Road jogger. Hikers on the Heron Trail have also encountered this mysterious spirit. The trail and the road intersect near Mount Hamilton Road. It is in that area where hikers have reported supernatural experiences.

One hiker reported a face-to-face encounter with the ghost. As the hiker looked into the jogger's face, he felt a strange sensation overcome his body. The hiker said it felt as if the jogger had looked "directly into his soul." Before the hiker could react, the ghostly vision turned around and jogged away.

The hiker is not the only person on the Heron Trail who has encountered the entity. Some who have seen him claim their bodies began to shake with fear at the sight of the ghost. Others became physically sick, as if they had suddenly come down with a virus or terrible fever.

Just who this otherworldly jogger is remains a mystery.

Quimby Road is a dangerous one, and many accidents there have resulted in the deaths of cyclists, hikers, and drivers. But the jogger has been running along that treacherous stretch of road as far back as anyone can remember, long before those deaths occurred. So just who is this mysterious jogger? And why is he spending the afterlife running on Quimby Road?

It is likely we will never know. What we can say for certain is, should you ever encounter him, it's probably best to let this jogger continue running on his own.

The Horrifying Hacienda Cemetery

Warning: This story is scary. Very scary. If I were you, I would not read this story before bedtime. Or if you are home alone. Or maybe ever.

Well, it looks like you are still reading, so prepare to be terrified.

There might not be any place in Santa Clara County quite as spooky as the Hacienda Cemetery in New Almaden. The dead have been resting there since the 1850s, but they do not rest peacefully.

The problems started back in 1928, when a man named Ben Black bought some land near the cemetery. He wanted to use Bertram Road to reach his new property, but the road did not extend that far. So, he filed a request with the city to make Bertram Road longer.

He waited and waited for the city to grant him permission to start the work. Then he waited some more. Finally, he grew impatient waiting for the city's answer. Unwilling to

wait any longer, Ben took matters into his own hands.

Late one night, Ben fired up his bulldozer. He was going to make his own extension to Bertram Road. There was just one problem—the graveyard was between the end of Bertram Road and Ben's land.

Well, that might have been a problem for you or me. But it didn't stop Ben.

The moonlight shone on the gravestones as Ben drove his bulldozer to the edge of the Hacienda Cemetery. He revved the engine.

He lowered the wide, steel blade at the front of the machine. He heard the dull thud of the blade landing in the grass. Then he began clearing a pathway from his new tract of land to Bertram Road.

Ben drove over an unknown number of graves that night. He could hear the crunch of gravestones under the wheels of the bulldozer, but he kept his foot on the gas pedal. Ben was determined to reach Bertram Road and nothing, not even the bodies of dead miners

and well-respected former residents, would stop him.

Ben created a new road that night. But the consequences of his actions can still be felt to this day.

If you look at a map, you'll see that Bertram Road still divides Hacienda Cemetery. The road is a bumpy one. Residents say that the bumps you feel as you drive down the road are the graves Ben Black demolished all those years ago. Each bump in the road is there to remind you that a grave lies just under the surface. The dead who rest there refuse to be forgotten, even though their tombstones are long gone.

However, it is not just the graves under the road that cause people to believe Hacienda Cemetery is haunted.

According to Kitty Monahan, longtime resident of New Almaden and president of the New Almaden Quicksilver County Park

Association, the cemetery used to be much larger than it is now. The thing is, none of the bodies that were buried in the original cemetery were relocated when the land started to be used for other things, like plots for new houses. That means it is very likely that some of the homes in the area have long-forgotten graves beneath them.

If that doesn't send a shiver up your spine, this might.

For years, the creek that runs alongside the Hacienda Cemetery was known to flood. When that happened, water would rush toward the cemetery. More than once, the water loosened the ground enough to release a long-ago buried body and send it floating down the river. The city of San Jose has since fixed the problem, but imagine the terror of seeing a corpse float past you—not to mention the restless spirits the river likely unleashed!

Not scared yet? Then read on.

In 1893, a thirteen-year-old boy named Richard Bertram Barrett lived in the area. Everyone called him Bert. One day, Bert was in a hunting accident. He survived, but he lost his left arm. His family decided to bury the arm in Hacienda Cemetery.

They dug a hole in the graveyard and placed the boy's arm inside. Then, they built a white wooden picket fence around the small grave. As a final step, the family pounded a wooden grave marker into the ground. The words carved into the wood read: "Richard Bertram 'Bert' Barrett. His arm lies here. 1893. May it rest in peace."

But that arm did not rest in peace, and the picket fence surrounding the arm's grave does nothing to keep the restless arm buried beneath the ground.

Bert lived to be seventy-nine years old.

When he died, his body (minus his left arm) was buried in Oak Hill Memorial Park. The two cemeteries are eleven miles apart. It is believed that the arm, separated from Bert for sixty-six years, longs to be reunited with the rest of Bert's body.

Legend has it that each month, on the night of the full moon—and, of course, every Halloween—the arm seemingly comes to life.

Its long-dead fingers claw their way through the soil to reach the surface of the grave. Once the arm is free from the ground, it nimbly scales the picket fence, and scampers along the ground. With the moonlight to guide its way, the arm uses its fingers to crawl past the other graves.

Most believe the arm is looking for Bert. But some think the arm doesn't just want to rejoin the body it lived with for thirteen years. They think the left arm searches for its missing body to bring Bert's body back to life!

Terrified yet? Don't say I didn't warn you!

The Hacienda Cemetery is open for visitors. That is, if you dare to walk among the restless spirits that call this graveyard home!

CHAPTER 9

Maxine's House

When you imagine a haunted house, what do you see in your mind? Is it a dark, gloomy mansion surrounded by a black wrought iron fence with a creaky gate? Are some of the windows broken? Is the yard overgrown?

What if I told you that some haunted houses look exactly like every other house on a pretty residential street? Sometimes, they look just like the house right next door to you.

This story is about a house that looks fine from the outside. But as we already know, looks can be deceiving.

There is a small, one-story home in the Doerr-Steindorf neighborhood of San Jose, where an old woman named Maxine lived for many years. She lived all alone, and all she had to keep her company was her collection of knickknacks and other trinkets. She filled her home with so many small collectibles that she barely had room for herself.

Maxine's neighbors worried about her being all alone in her house. Maxine was sweet and

neighborly, but she was obviously very lonely. The neighbors would occasionally check on her to make sure she was well and safe. When no had seen or heard from Maxine for a few days, the neighbors called the police. The police discovered that Maxine had died some time before, surrounded by her trinkets and knickknacks.

In time, all of Maxine's collectibles were removed from the home. It was fixed up and ready for the next people to move in. That couple was Windy and Doug.

When the couple moved into the home, it was a restful place. They were happy in the home. Eventually, the couple decided to add a baby to the family.

When their newborn baby Jack came home from the hospital, strange things started to happen. It seemed like new parents were always losing things, and then finding them in the strangest places. They would hear unexplained noises coming from empty rooms.

They didn't know exactly what was happening until Jack grew a little older.

Jack had a habit of chattering to himself in his crib when he was put down at night, or when he was supposed to be napping. One day, Jack told his mother that he wasn't talking to himself. He was talking to his friend, Max.

Windy's blood ran cold when she heard what the little boy said. She knew exactly who Jack had been talking to. The neighbors had told her about Maxine when the couple first moved in. She knew Maxine had died inside the home. Now she realized that the old woman was still there!

Once Windy and Doug discovered that Maxine's spirit was still in the house, the ghost began to interact with them as well.

Maxine likes to hide small kitchen tools and pieces of jewelry from Windy. The small items will mysteriously show up in other rooms, in different drawers, and other places no one would think to look. Who else but Maxine would put a potato peeler in the sock drawer?

The good news is, this ghost isn't malicious. If Windy can't locate something that Maxine has hidden, she will calmly ask the specter to return the item to her. Maxine always complies.

But Maxine has been known to lose her temper. If something is happening in the house that the ghostly woman does not like, she lets the family know. She usually does this by knocking things off walls and pushing things over to create a clatter.

Maxine might like Windy and Doug, but she loves Jack. The two spent a great deal of time together when Jack was a baby. When he was young, the boy seemed to love Maxine as much as the ghostly woman loved him. But as Jack got older, her visits to him grew more disturbing.

Eventually, Jack grew frightened of the ghost that always seemed to be around him. The boy asked Maxine to go away many times, but she would never stay away for very long.

Maxine most often comes to spend time with the boy at night. Sometimes she will appear in Jack's dreams. Other times she will be in the room when he wakes from the dream. Maxine won't leave the boy alone, so he has learned to live with her otherworldly presence.

Maxine, who was so lonely in life, is now

surrounded by a loving family. But this joy for Maxine will not last much longer.

The family has lived with Maxine for fifteen years. Soon, it will be time for Windy, Doug, and Jack to move to a new home. The family believes that Maxine knows her time with them is coming to an end. The ghost has become less active as the family makes arrangements to leave the home.

Windy hopes the next family to move into Maxine's house will be as welcoming and understanding of the spirit as her family has been. If they aren't, Windy hopes they adapt quickly to having one extra family member. Because she is certain that Maxine has no intention of leaving the home she occupied in life. And still does, long after her death.

A Ghostly Goodbye

Thanks for exploring the spooky side of San Jose with us. From the world-famous Winchester Mystery House® to eerily empty roads in the foothills, ghosts seem to be everywhere in California's third largest city! All of this ghost talk might have caused you to hide under the covers and keep a light on at night. Or, maybe you are inspired to become a paranormal investigator and try out some ghost hunting of your own.

If you *do* decide to go exploring in hopes of having your own ghostly encounter, watch out—you just might get more than you bargained for! After all, ghosts that seem a *little* spooky in the book, just might be TERRIFYING in real life!

Remember to stick only to places you are allowed to enter, and always get permission from a trusted adult before you go ghost hunting. Most importantly, make sure your

ghostly adventure is a safe one. Stay in a group, take notes, and always—and I do mean ALWAYS!—watch your back. Because in spooky San Jose, you never know just who, or what, might be right behind you!